A Stake In The Game

The Role of SkinDaily Life's Unexpected Asymmetries

By

David M. McGuire

Table of contents

Introduction

The Incerto collection consists of a combination of a) real-world discussions, b) philosophical stories, and c) scientific and analytical commentary on the problems of randomness, as well as how to live, eat, sleep, argue, fight, make friends, work, have fun, and make decisions under uncertainty, continues with this book, despite being a stand-alone. Don't be misled by the Incerto's accessibility—it is an essay, not a dull popularization of works done elsewhere in boring form (except the technical companion).

The four topics covered in Skin in the Game are a) uncertainty and the validity of knowledge (both practical and scientific, assuming there is a difference); or, in less polite terms, "bulls**t detection"; b) symmetry in human affairs, which refers to fairness, justice, responsibility, and reciprocity; c) information sharing in transactions; and d) rationality in complex systems and everyday life. When one has "skin in the game," it is clear that these four cannot be separated. -

Skin in the game is essential for more than simple justice, business efficiency, and risk management; it's also essential for understanding how the world works.

First, it involves recognizing and removing bullsh*t, or the distinction between theory and practice, superficial and genuine competence, and academia (in the negative meaning of the term) and the outside world. According to Yogiberrism, there is no distinction between the actual world and academia in the academic setting, but there is in the latter.
In reality, symmetry and reciprocity are distorted in such a way that if you want the benefits, you must also accept certain risks to avoid making other people pay for your errors. You must pay a price if you put others in danger and they suffer as a result. In the same manner that you should treat people as you want to be treated, you want to share responsibility for events fairly and equally.
If you express an opinion and someone acts on it, you are ethically required to experience the consequences of that action. If you're sharing your opinions on the economy, simply tell me what's in your portfolio rather than what you "think."
The book also discusses what a used car dealer should and shouldn't tell you about the automobile you're about to invest a significant portion of your funds. The third topic covered in the book is how much knowledge one should share with others.

Fourth, it has to do with logic and standing the test of time. Real-world rationality has nothing to do with what makes sense to your New Yorker writer or a psychologist employing simplistic first-order models; rather, it has to do with something statistically much more complex and related to your survival.

Do not confuse having skin in the game—as it is described here and utilized in this book—with simply an incentive issue or a portion of the rewards (as it is commonly understood in finance). No. It is more about having a fair share of the damage and paying a price if anything goes wrong than it is about symmetry. The same concept connects concepts such as incentives, purchasing a used automobile, ethics, contract theory, learning (real world vs. academic), Kantian imperative, municipal authority, risk science, and more. Do not confuse having skin in the game—as it is described here and utilized in this book—with simply an incentive issue or a portion of the rewards (as it is commonly understood in finance). No. It is more about having a fair share of the damage and paying a price if anything goes wrong than it is about symmetry. The same concept connects concepts such as incentives, buying used cars, ethics, contract theory, learning (real-life vs. academia), Kantian imperative, municipal power, risk science, contact between intellectuals and reality, the accountability of bureaucrats, probabilistic social justice, option theory, upright behavior, bullk**t vendors, theology, and let's stop there for the moment.

THE GAME'S LESS OBVIOUS SKIN DETAILS

The title of the book should have been The Less Obvious Aspects of Skin in the Game: Those Hidden Asymmetries and Their Consequences, which is more accurate (though less catchy). Because I just dislike reading books that point out the obvious, I like being shocked. As a result, I won't force the reader into a tedious, predictable trip as in a college lecture, but rather into the kind of experience I'd want to have.

structured in the way shown below. The reader will understand the significance, pervasiveness, and ubiquitous nature of the skin in the game (that is, symmetry) in most of its features after reading no more than roughly sixty pages. A principle is debased by continuously defending it, therefore avoid giving elaborate explanations of why something is vital.

The less boring path involves concentrating on the second step: the unexpected implications—those hidden asymmetries that do not immediately spring to mind—as well as the less apparent repercussions, some of which are rather disagreeable, and many of which are surprisingly beneficial. Understanding how the skin works in the game enables us to comprehend complex problems hiding behind reality's fine-grained grid.

For example: How do the world's most intolerable minority rule and dictate our tastes? How does universalism harm those whom it purports to serve? How is it that there are now more slaves than there were throughout the Roman era? Why shouldn't doctors have doctor-like appearances? Why did Christian theology continue to emphasize that Jesus Christ had a human component that must be separate from the divine?

How can historians mislead us by writing about war instead of peace? How is it that risk-free, low-cost signaling fails in both social and religious contexts? Why do bureaucrats with perfect qualifications appear more credible than political candidates with glaring character flaws? We revere Hannibal, but why? How can businesses fail the moment they have qualified management who want to achieve well?

How can paganism have a greater symmetry across demographics? How should international relations be handled? Why should you never contribute to established charities unless they are highly distributive (or, in more recent parlance, "Uberized")? Why do genes propagate differently than languages? Why does the size of communities matter (a community of fishermen becomes antagonistic if the scale, or the total number of participants, is raised a notch)? Why do markets have nothing to do with participant biases and behavioral economics have little to do with the study of human behavior? How can reason ensure its survival? What is the fundamental justification for taking on risk? But according to this author, having skin in the game is primarily about concepts like fairness, honor, and sacrifice that are essential to human existence.

Generally speaking, applying the principle of skin in the game lessens the effects of the following divergences that emerged with civilization: those between action and cheap talk (talk), consequence and Coventry and Brussels, Omaha and Washington, D.C., merchant and bureaucrat, genuine and cosmetic, strong and display, love and gold-digging, intention, practice and theory, honor and reputation,

expertise and charlatanism, concrete and abstract, ethical and legal, genuine and genuine, entrepreneur and chief executive, merchant and bureaucrat.
Just to offer a sense of how the concept transcends categories, let's first connect a few dots of the elements in the aforementioned list with two vignettes.
Consider the following to see why ethics, moral responsibilities, and talents cannot be clearly distinguished in real life. Do you mean that you trust someone's integrity (he won't transfer money to Panama) when you say, "I trust you," to someone in a position of responsibility, like your bookkeeper, or do you mean that you trust both? The fundamental idea of the book is that it is difficult to separate knowledge and ability from ethics in the actual world.

Chapter 1

Equality in Uncertainty: Why Everyone Should Eat Their Turtles

The phrase first appeared in the following context. Several turtles were allegedly captured by a group of fishermen. After boiling them, they discovered that these marine creatures were considerably less palatable than they had assumed since few people in the party were ready to consume them. Mercury, who was the god of commerce, abundance, messengers, and the underworld, as well as the patron of thieves and brigands and, unsurprisingly, luck, happened to be passing by. Mercury was the most multifaceted, somewhat organized god. He was allowed to join the gang and eat the turtles. He made them all eat the turtles after realizing that he had been invited merely to get rid of the food they didn't want, thereby creating the idea that you should consume what you serve others.

A Client is Born I've gained knowledge from my own inexperienced mistakes every day.

Be wary of anybody who offers counsel by informing you that a specific course of action is "good for you" even when it is also beneficial to him and the damage to you doesn't directly affect him.

Of course, such counsel is often given uninvited. The asymmetry occurs when the advice is given to you but not to him. He may be attempting to sell you something, get you to wed his daughter, or convince you to work for his son-in-law.

I got a letter from a lecture agency years ago. His letter was straightforward; it contained about ten inquiries of the form "do you have the time to field requests?", "Can you manage the planning of the trip," and the like, with the fundamental premise being that a lecture agent would improve my life and allow me to pursue knowledge or whatever else I was interested in while the responsibility for the details falls on someone else. And it wasn't just any lecture agent; only he was capable of all of these things; he reads books and has access to intellectuals' minds (at the time, I didn't find the term "intellectual" offensive). I immediately sensed trouble because, as is customary with those who provide unsolicited advice, he never shied away from telling me outright or implying that it was "good for me" at any point in the conversation.

Even though I didn't buy into the reasoning, I was a fool and agreed to conduct business with him by giving him control of a booking in the nation where he had his base of operations. Everything was well until I got a letter from the country's tax officials six years later. I got in touch with him right away to ask whether any other American citizens he had recruited had had a similar tax difficulty or if he had heard of any other such circumstances. He immediately responded with the harsh, "I am not your tax attorney," refusing to say if any other American clients who had engaged him because it was "good for them" had had a similar issue.

It always turns out that what is portrayed as being beneficial for you is excellent for the other side in the roughly a dozen instances I can recall. As a trader, you learn to recognize and deal with morally upright individuals, those who approach you with a product to offer and clarify that the transaction is taking place for their gain by asking, "Do you have an axe?" (meaning an inquiry whether you have a certain interest). Avoid at all costs anybody who calls you to promote a specific product under the cover of guidance and tries to sell you merchandise. In actuality, the turtle's tale serves as a template for human interactions throughout history.

I formerly worked for a famous U.S. investment firm, known as "white shoe" because its partners were members of exclusive golf clubs where they participated in the sport while wearing white shoes. Like all such businesses, a reputation for integrity and professionalism was fostered, reinforced, and safeguarded. However, on days when they wore black shoes, salespeople (really, salesmen) had the duty of "unloading" inventory, namely securities that traders were "stuffed" with but needed to get rid of to reduce their risk profile. Selling to other dealers was out of the question because they would scent surplus inventory and drive down the price. Professional traders are usually not golfers. Some dealers offered variable pay to the sales force in the form of (%) "points," which rose in value as we were more eager to sell stocks. Salesmen would take customers out to dinner, buy them pricey wine (typically the most expensive option on the menu), and then dump the undesired items on them to make a handsome profit on the hundreds of dollars in restaurant bills. I once had a professional salesperson tell me in no uncertain terms: "If I buy the customer, working for the finance department of a municipality, who purchases his clothes from some department shop in New Jersey, a bottle of $2,000 wine, I own him for the next several months. I'll be able to make at least $100,000 off of him.

Nothing like it is available on the market. The client who paid more than $100,000 for a $2,000 bottle of wine is a New Jersey resident who is presently retired and whose job included overseeing a pension fund for public employees.

The age-old query, "Is it moral to sell something to someone knowing the price would soon decline," has an equally simple answer. The controversy dates back to a discussion between two stoic philosophers—Diogenes of Babylon and his follower Antipater of Tarsus—who adopted the higher moral position based on asymmetric knowledge and seems to align with the contemporary ethics supported by this author. The works of neither author are complete, but we do know a lot through secondary—or, in the case of Cicero, tertiary—sources. Cicero posed the following question in his work De Officiis. Assume that during a period of scarcity and hunger in Rhodes, a man transported a large quantity of maize from Alexandria to Rhodes. Imagine that he was also aware that many vessels carrying comparable goods had left Alexandria for Rhodes. He had to tell the Rhodians, right? In these situations, how may one behave honorably or dishonorably?

We traders had a simple response. Selling amounts to customers without disclosing the existence of substantial stocks that are ready to be sold is what we referred to as "stuffing." An honorable dealer wouldn't treat other experienced traders that way; it was improper. The objection was the punishment. However, doing it to the faceless nontraders and the anonymous market, sometimes known as "the Swiss," or some distant fool, was kind of OK. With certain individuals, we have a relational rapport, but with others, we just have a transactional one. The two were divided by an ethical barrier, similar to how domestic animals could not be mistreated but cockroaches were exempt from the cruelty laws.

According to Diogenes, the vendor must provide as much disclosure as permitted by civil law. According to Antipater, everything should be provided, above and above what is required by law, to ensure that neither the seller nor the buyer is in the dark about any information.

Antipater's perspective is stronger since it is independent of context, circumstance, time, and the participant's eye color. let's assume that

Always, the ethical is more durable than the legal. The legal and ethical should always converge over time, never the other way around.

hence:

Laws change, but morality never does.

Because the concept of "law" is nebulous and very context-specific, such disclosures are included in U.S. civil law owing to consumer activists and related movements, but other nations have different legislation. This is especially evident concerning securities laws, since in the U.S. disclosure of insider knowledge and "front running" restrictions are both necessary, but in Europe, they previously weren't.

A large portion of the job done by investment banks in my time was to manipulate rules and look for legal loopholes. And, strangely enough, the more rules there were, the simpler it was to generate money.

Insecurity and Equity

This brings up asymmetry, which is the fundamental idea underlying skin in the game. The issue that arises is: to what degree may parties to a transaction have various levels of information? The ancient

Mediterranean and, to a certain degree, the contemporary world seem to be moving in the direction of Antipater's viewpoint. Although "buyer beware" (caveat emptor) is a legal phrase in the Anglo-Saxon West, it is very recent, seldom broad, and often tempered by lemon laws. (A "lemon" is now a broad term that refers to pretty much everything that moves; initially, a "lemon" was a persistently faulty automobile; for example, my convertible Mini, in love with the garage.

The world is moving toward Diogenes' position of transparency, not necessarily through regulations as much as thanks to tort laws, which allow one to sue for damages if the seller misled them. Cicero asked this question in the debate between the two ancient stoics, "If a man knowingly offers for sale wine that is spoiling, ought he to tell his customers? It's important to keep in mind that tort laws give the seller a stake in the result; this is why companies hate and abhor them. However, tort laws have drawbacks and should only be applied in a non-native fashion, that is, in a way that makes them impossible to manipulate. They will be manipulated, as we shall see when we talk about the medical appointment.

We are interested in Sharia, namely the rule governing Islamic banking and transactions since it maintains certain long-lost Babylonian and Mediterranean practices—not to boost the ego of Saudi princes. It serves as a storehouse for all ancient Mediterranean and Semitic knowledge since it sits at the confluence of Greco-Roman law (as seen by their interactions with the School of Law at Berytus), Phoenician trade laws, Babylonian laws, and Arab tribe commercial practices. As a result, I see Sharia as a repository of theories about symmetry in transactions. Sharia imposes the Gharar injunction, which is so severe as to be completely prohibited in all forms of transaction. It is a very complex decision theory phrase with no equivalent in English; it denotes both uncertainty and deceit. In my opinion, it also denotes something other than an informational imbalance between agents. It denotes uncertainty inequality. Simply put, an imbalance becomes theft since the goal of a transaction is for both parties to face random outcomes with the same uncertainty. Or more forcefully:

In a transaction, neither party should be assured of the result while the other is doubtful.

Like any juridical phrase, Gharar has a drawback; it is still less effective than Antipater's strategy. Sharia is broken if just one participant in a transaction is certain from beginning to end. However, if there is just a little asymmetry—for example, if someone has insider knowledge that provides them an advantage in the markets—there is no Gharar since there is still enough uncertainty for both parties because the price is unpredictable. After all, only God knows the future. Selling a faulty product, on the other hand, is against the law. Therefore, whereas the second situation, involving a faulty beverage, might, the vendor of grain in Rhodes knowing does not fall under Gharar in my first example.

As we can see, the issue of asymmetry is so complex that several schools provide various ethical answers; thus, let's examine the Talmudic perspective.

In this regard, Rav Safra and Swiss Jewish ethics are more like Diogenes than Antipater; in fact, they strive for more openness than Diogenes. Not only should there be openness about the product, but there may also need to be one regarding the seller's intentions and inner thoughts. The following incident is related to the medieval rabbi known as

"Rashi," Rabbi Shlomo Yitzhaki (also known as Salomon Isaacides). A businessman and scholar from Babylonia in the third century, Rav Safra, was selling certain products. When a buyer attempted to acquire the goods at an initial price while he was silently praying and the Rabbi did not respond, the buyer upped the price. However, Rav Safra believed that he had to uphold the original goal and had no intention of selling for more than the first amount. Is Rav Safra required to sell at the original price, or should he accept the increased one? [v] [vi]

In what seems to be a competitive world of transactions, such complete openness is not ludicrous nor unusual. This was true in my old world of trading. As a trader who has regularly encountered that issue, I will support Rav Safra's position in this argument. Let's go logically. Remember how the chapter's previous salesmen were rapacious? Sometimes I would interact with a customer via a salesman and offer something for sale for, say, $5, but the salesperson would respond with an "upgrade" of $5.10. The additional ten cents never seemed quite right. Simply put, it was not a viable business model. What if the client later learned that my original offer was $5? The humiliation is not worth any reward. The practice of "stuffing" consumers with inferior goods and overcharging belongs in the same category. Now, to relate this to Rav Safra's tale, what if he sold the same thing to one customer at the markup price and to a different customer at the original price, and the two customers just so happened to know one another? What if they represented the same end user as agents?

The most successful, shame-free policy is maximum openness, including transparency of goals, even if it may not be morally obligatory.

The narrative leaves out the fact that the buyer may have been one of those "Swiss," or foreigners, to whom our moral standards do not apply. There I will be a species for whom our moral standards would be loosened or perhaps abandoned. Otherwise, the system cannot operate as intended, as Eleanor Ostrom recently demonstrated.

Members as well as Non-Members

Because it is not insignificant to exclude "Swiss" from our ethical standards. Because things don't "scale" and generalize, I find it difficult to understand when intellectuals discuss abstract concepts. A nation is not a big city, a city is not a big family, and the whole planet is not a big village,

I'm sorry to say. We will talk about scale transformations here and in a separate, more technical chapter in Section X at the conclusion.

When Athenians debate "democracy," they only apply it to other citizens, not slaves or metics, and they regard all viewpoints equally (the equivalent of green card or J1b visa holders). Theodosius' law effectively denied Roman citizens who wed "Barbarians" their legal rights, denying them ethical equivalence with other people. They were expelled from the club. Jewish ethics makes a distinction between thick and thin blood: while we are all related, some of us are more related than others[3].

People have historically belonged to organizations with rules and member conduct like those of modern country clubs, both inside and out. Club members are aware that exclusivity and size restrictions are inherent to the very nature of clubs. Spartans were supposed to die for their own sake and the good of Sparta, and they could hunt and kill helots—non-citizens who were treated as slaves for training—but they were otherwise equal to other Spartans. There were many fraternities, clubs, open and (often) secret groups, and even funeral clubs where members contributed to the burial expenses and took part in the rituals in the main towns of the pre-

Christian ancient world, notably in the Levant and Asia Minor.

The modern Roma population, often known as gypsies, has very rigorous norms of conduct for both themselves and the dirty non-gypsies known as payos. And because of the partnership structure of governance, even the investment firm Goldman Sachs, famed for its ruthless cupidity, behaves like a communist commune from the inside, as the anthropologist David Graeber has noted.

So we follow our moral principles, but there is a limit—from scaling—beyond which the principles are no longer applicable. Unfortunately, the general kills the specific. Is it feasible to be both ethical and universalist? is an issue that we shall revisit after a more in-depth consideration of complexity theory. Tragically, in reality, not so much. Because when "us" becomes too big a group, things deteriorate and everyone begins looking out for themselves. For us, the abstract is simply too abstract. In contrast to the contrary, which has failed with bigger governments, I like political systems that start at the local level and work their way up (ironically, those that are "Swiss"). Being somewhat tribal is not a terrible thing, and instead of combining all tribes into one big soup, we need to work in a fractal approach to establish healthy relationships between tribes. In that regard, federalism modeled after the United States is ideal.

My pessimism about unrestricted globalization and massive, centralized multiethnic nations stems from this scale transition from the specific to the generic. My study partner Yaneer Bar-Yam, a physicist and complexity researcher, demonstrated that "better fences meant better neighbors"—a concept that local governments and "policymakers" alike find difficult to comprehend when it comes to the Near East. I shall reiterate scaling issues till my voice becomes hoarse. The attempt to bring Shiites, Christians, and Sunnis together and urge them to hold hands and sing Kumbaya around a campfire in the name of human unity and fraternity has failed (interventionists aren't yet aware that "should" isn't a strong enough empirical claim to "create countries"). One of the stupidities of interventionists is blaming people for being "sectarian" rather than capitalizing on such a natural propensity. Tribes may be officially divided (like the Ottomans did) or simply marked off with markings to bring them together.

However, we don't have to go far to understand the significance of scaling. Neighbors get along better than roommates.

When you consider it, it is evident—even trite—from the well-known differences in crowd behavior between those in large cities and those in small towns. I sometimes visit the hamlet of my ancestors, which has a family-like atmosphere. People help out, care about their neighbor, even if they despise his dog, and visit other people's funerals (funeral clubs were largely in big cities). When the other person is a hypothetical entity and our conduct toward them is regulated by some general ethical guideline, rather than someone in flesh and blood, it is impossible to achieve the same cohesiveness in a bigger metropolis. When seen in that light, we understand it quickly but fail to recognize that ethics is an essentially local concept.

Greek is a precise language and contains a term for risk sharing, which is the reverse of risk transfer. All (Literally) in the Same Boat Synkyndineo, which is Greek for "taking risks jointly," was necessary for marine trade.

The journey of St. Paul aboard a cargo ship from Sidon via Crete to Malta is described in The Acts of the Apostles[5]. When they had had their fill, they "lightened the ship by tossing the maize out into the water" as they approached a storm.

Now, not only the individual owners but all owners were to share in the expenses of the lost items while they were being ejected. Because it turned out that they were according to a tradition that was documented in Lex Rhodia, often known as Rhodian Law, named after the commercial island of Rhodes in the Aegean Sea, but which goes back to at least 800 B.C. It mandates that risks and expenses for eventualities must be borne equally, without regard to blame. Here's how Justinian's code[6] puts it:

The Rhodian Law stipulates that in cases when goods are thrown overboard to lighten a ship, what has been lost must be made up for by contributions from all parties.

The same system of risk sharing is also applied to caravans traveling through desert roads. All merchants, not just the owner, had to share the expenses of lost or stolen goods.

How Not to Become a Doctor

While necessary, attempts to integrate personal risk into medicine often have a specific class of negative consequences by moving uncertainty from the clinician to the patient.

The regulatory framework and legal framework are likely to place the doctor's skin in the wrong game. How? The over-reliance on metrics is the issue. Every parameter may be manipulated; the cholesterol-lowering strategy we outlined in the Prologue is an extreme example of this. What kind of therapy would a cancer doctor or hospital choose to conduct if, more realistically, they were assessed on the five-year survival rates of their patients and had to choose from several modalities for a new patient? Laser surgery (a surgical technique) and radiation treatment, which is hazardous to the patient as well as cancer, are trade-offs. In terms of statistics, radiation treatment may result in poorer five-year results than laser surgery, but the latter has a propensity to cause secondary cancers in the long run and gives a relatively lower twenty-year disease-specific survival. The temptation is to aim for the former since the computation of patient survival is done over a five-year timeframe rather than a twenty-year window.

By choosing the second-best course of action, the doctor is most likely trying to remove some of the ambiguity from himself or herself.

The system forces a doctor to shift risk from himself to you and from the here and now to the future.

And in the situation, we already observed, from the far future.

When you enter a doctor's office, keep in mind that despite his authoritative manner, the person you will be dealing with is vulnerable. He has no immediate emotional loss should your health deteriorate since he is not you or a member of your family. Naturally, he wants to avoid a lawsuit since it may be bad for his career.

You can die from some measurements. Let's assume you see a cardiologist and discover that you fall into the category of moderate risk, which doesn't increase your chance of a cardiovascular event but signals the beginning of a potentially concerning disease. A prediabetic or prehypertensive individual is 90% closer to a normal person than to someone who has the ailment (there is a substantial nonlinearity). But to defend himself, the doctor feels compelled to treat you. In the unlikely event that you pass away straight away after the appointment, the doctor may be held liable for negligence for not prescribing the proper medication, such as statins, which were formerly thought to be helpful but are now known to have been supported by questionable or insufficient research. He could be aware, deep down, that taking a statin would have negative long-term implications. However, the pharmaceutical industry has succeeded in convincing everyone that these unintended effects are innocuous while the prudent course of action is to see the unknown as potentially hazardous. In reality, the hazards exceed the benefits for most individuals, except for those who are very sick. The difference between the dangers and the legal risk is that the hazards are concealed and will manifest over time. This is similar to Bob Rubin's risk transfer strategy, which delays hazards and makes them seem undetectable.

Can one lessen the asymmetry in medicine now? The answer, I have argued in Antifragile and more precisely elsewhere, is for the patient to forgo therapy while they are just moderately unwell and only utilize the medication for "tail events," or for seldom occurring serious diseases. Pharmaceutical firms have an incentive to concentrate on the "mildly" unwell since they make up a bigger population than the seriously ill and are anticipated to live longer and use medications for longer.

In conclusion, administrators lack skin in the game, and they seem to be the root of the system's worrying malfunctions. Both the doctor and the patient have stakes in the outcome, albeit not always equally. All around the world and throughout history, administrators have been a scourge.

Chapter 2:

The Dominance of the Stubborn Minority: The Most Intolerant Wins.

The following scenario is the finest illustration of a complicated system's operation that I am aware of. A certain kind of intransigent minority just has to make up a tiny fraction of the population—say, three or four percent—for the rest of the population to be forced to accept their choices. Furthermore, the minority's dominance creates an optical illusion, giving the appearance that the majority's preferences and decisions are what is being made. The reason it looks silly is that our scientific intuitions aren't calibrated for it (fudged about academic and scientific intuitions and hasty judgments; they don't work and your typical intellectualization fails with complicated systems, but not your grandmothers' wisdom).

The fundamental tenet of complex systems is that the ensemble exhibits behavior that is unanticipated by the individual parts. More important than a unit's essence are its relationships. It is reasonable to state that studying a single and will never, ever provide us with insight into how the ant colony functions. To do so, it is necessary to comprehend that an ant colony is just that—a colony of ants—nothing more, nothing less. This is referred to as an "emergent" quality of the whole, in which the interactions between these elements are what distinguish the whole from its parts. Furthermore, interactions might follow very basic norms. The minority rule is the rule we examine in this chapter.

The minority rule will demonstrate how all it takes for society to run well is a tiny number of intolerant, morally upright individuals with skin in the game, in the form of bravery.

Ironically, I was attending the summer BBQ for the New England Complex Systems institute when this complexity example struck me. The guests' observant buddy who only ate Kosher walked over to say hi as they were setting up the table and unloading the beverages. I almost expected him to turn down the glass of yellow sugared water with citric acid that I offered him because of his dietary restrictions. He refused. Another Kosher individual said, "Liquids around here are Kosher," as he sipped the lemonade. We had a peek at the carton package. It said it was Kosher in very small lettering with a tiny symbol, a U within a circle. Those who need to know and are looking for the tiny print will see the emblem. As for me, I had been speaking in the third person all these years without realizing it and consuming Kosher beverages without realizing they were Kosher.

Figure 3 shows a container of lemonade with the letter U circled to denote that it is (literally) Kosher.

Criminals who are allergic to peanuts

I had an odd thought. Less than three-tenths of one percent of American citizens identify as Kosher. However, it seems that practically all beverages are kosher. Why? For no other reason than that adopting fully kosher frees up the manufacturer, retailer, and restaurant from having to identify liquids as kosher or nonkosher using special markers, separate aisles, separate inventory, and various stocking sub-facilities. And the following is the straightforward rule that modifies the sum:

A nonkosher eater is not prohibited from consuming kosher food, but a kosher (or halal) eater will never consume nonkosher (or nonhalal) food.

A handicapped person won't use the usual restroom, but a non-disabled person will use the restroom designated for disabled persons, to put it another way.

Granted, sometimes in reality we hesitate to use the restroom with the disability sign on it because of a little misunderstanding - misinterpret the regulation for parking automobiles, believing that the restroom is just for the use of the disabled.

While a person without a peanut allergy may eat goods that have no traces of peanuts in them, someone with a peanut allergy will not be able to consume such products.

Which explains why it is so difficult to find peanuts on flights and why it is prohibited to eat peanuts in schools (which, in a sense, increases the number of people who have peanut allergies since decreased exposure is one of the causes of such allergies).

Let's put the principle into practice in several amusing fields:

While a criminal will quickly participate in lawful activity, an honest individual would never do so.

Let's refer to this minority as being intransigent and the majority as being flexible. Asymmetries in selections are the norm.

Once I played a joke on a buddy. New York had smoking and nonsmoking areas in restaurants years ago when Big Tobacco was concealing and suppressing the evidence of danger from secondary smoking (even outrageously, aircraft had a smoking section). I once took a buddy who was visiting from

Europe out to lunch, but we were only able to eat in the smoking areas of the restaurant. I persuaded my companion that because we had to smoke in the smoking area, we needed to purchase cigarettes. He gave in.

A further two items. First, the spatial organization of the terrain, or topography, plays a role. It makes a great difference whether the intransigents are isolated in their area or mixed in with the general population. The minority rule would not be applicable if the followers of the minority lived in Ghettos with their little economies. The (flexible) majority will have to submit to the minority's rule, however, when a population has an even spatial distribution, such as when the ratio of a minority in a neighborhood is the same as that in the village, the village is the same as in the county, the county is the same as in the state, and the state is the same as nationwide.

The cost structure is also very important. In our first example, adding Kosher certification to lemonade doesn't significantly alter the price, making inventory unnecessary. However, if producing Kosher lemonade was much more expensive, the rule would be reduced in a nonlinear relation to the cost differential. The minority rule won't apply if making Kosher food costs 10 times as much, with the possible exception of a few affluent districts.

So to speak, Muslims have Kosher regulations, although they are far more restrictive and only apply to meat. Muslims and Jews follow very similar laws on animal slaughter (all Kosher is halal for the majority of Sunni Muslims, or was in ages past; the opposite is not true). Due to the skin-in-the-game mentality that originated in the ancient Eastern Mediterranean (described in Chapter), certain slaughter regulations should be noted. Greek and Semitic customs dictate that one should only worship the gods if they have anything to gain from doing so. Gods do not like shoddy signaling.

In the United Kingdom, where there is only three to four percent of (practicing) Muslims, a large majority of the meat is halal. The majority of the lamb imported from New Zealand is halal, at around 70%. Despite the substantial expenses associated with the lost revenue from non-pork establishments, less than 10% of the Subway chain's locations are halal-only (i.e., they do not serve pork). The same is true in South Africa, where a disproportionately greater percentage of chicken is Halal certified while having a similar percentage of Muslims. Halal, however, is not sufficiently neutral to achieve a high level in the UK and other Christian nations since individuals may exploit other people's religious conventions. For example, in his renowned rebellious lyric professing his Christianity, the Christian Arab poet Al-Akhtar from the 7th century said, "I do not consume sacrifice flesh."

As the Muslim population in Europe rises, it is reasonable to assume that the same rejection of Islamic standards will occur in the West.

Renormalization group in Figure 4: starting at the top, go through steps one through three:

Four boxes contain four boxes, with the first application of the minority rule turning one of the boxes pink.

Therefore, the minority rule may result in a higher proportion of halal food in the shops than is justified by the percentage of halal diners in the public. However, there may be a barrier since some individuals may have a taboo against eating food that is Muslim. However, with certain non-religious Kashrut regulations, so to speak, the percentage may be anticipated to converge to near 100%. (or some high number). Because of the minority rule and the possibility that regular, unlabeled food may include pesticides, herbicides, and transgenic genetically modified organisms, or "GMOs," with unknown hazards, some people in the U.S. and Europe are buying more and more "organic" food items. (In this sense, transgenic food, which involves the transfer of genes from an alien organism or species, is what we refer to as GMOs.) Or it can be due to existential concerns, caution, or Burkean conservatism; some people might not want to go too far from the foods their ancestors ate. Something may be declared to be "organic" if it is free of transgenic GMOs.

The huge agricultural businesses erroneously thought that all they needed to promote genetically modified food was to win over the majority. They did this by engaging in all kinds of lobbying, buying lawmakers, and overt scientific misinformation (including smear campaigns against people like me). You fools, no. As I have said, making judgments of this kind with hasty, "scientific" judgment is too foolish. Consider the fact that people who consume transgenic GMOs will not eat non-GMOs. For the whole population to be required to consume non-GMO food, it may be sufficient to have a little, say no more than 5%, the equally dispersed population of non-GMO eaters. How? Let's imagine that you are planning a corporate event, a wedding, or a lavish party to commemorate the overthrow of the Saudi Arabian government, the collapse of the rent-seeking investment bank Goldman Sachs, or the public vilification of Ray Kotcher, chairman of the public relations company Ketchum that smears scientists and scientific whistleblowers on behalf of large corporations. Do you need to send out a survey asking individuals whether they consume transgenic GMOs or not to plan customized meals? No. Simply choose anything that is non-GMO, provided that the price difference is not considerable. Because transportation and storage expenses account for up to 80% or 90% of the cost of (perishable) food in America rather than the cost of production at the agricultural level, the price difference seems to be insignificant. Additionally, because of the minority rule, distribution costs fall as demand for organic food (and products with labels like "natural") rises. As a result, the minority rule ends up increasing.

Big Ag (the huge agricultural businesses) was unaware that this was analogous to joining a game in which one needed to win not only more points than the opponent, but also 97% of all points to be safe. It is surprising to see Big Ag, which spent hundreds of millions of dollars on research and defamation campaigns, along with hundreds of academics who believe they are smarter than the average person, misunderstand such a basic concept as asymmetric choices.

Another illustration: Don't assume that the popularity of automatic-shifting automobiles is since most drivers originally preferred them; it might just be that those who can operate manual shifts can always use automatic, even if the reverse is not always true 21.

21 Gratitude to Amir-Reza Amini.

Renormalization group, a potent tool in mathematical physics that enables us to observe how things scale up, is the approach of analysis used in this case (or down). Next, let's study it without using math.

GROUP FOR RENORMALIZATION

Four boxes are shown in Figure 2 in a pattern known as fractal self-similarity. Four smaller boxes are included in every package. As we go up and down until we reach a particular level, each of the four boxes will contain four further boxes.

There are two options: pink for the minority preference and yellow for the majority decision.

Assume the smaller unit has a family of four, totaling four persons. One of them adheres to the intransigent minority and consumes exclusively organic and non-GMO foods. The box is pink, whereas the other objects are yellow. As we advance, we "renormalize once": the four are now ruled by the daughter's intransigence, and the unit has gone pink, meaning it will choose nonGMO. In the third phase, the family will attend a BBQ party where three other families will also be present. The visitors will only make organic food since they are known for only eating nonGMO food. The neighborhood's single nonGMO food shop converts to nonGMO to make life easier after discovering this, which affects the local wholesaler and causes the story to "renormalize."

By some strange coincidence, I was vacationing in New York the day before the Boston barbecue, and I stopped by the office of a friend I wanted to stop from working—that is, from engaging in an activity that, when misused, results in poor posture, a loss of definition in the facial features, and a loss of mental clarity. Serge Galam, a French physicist who was there by chance, passed the time at the friend's office. The primary book on the topic, which had been languishing for months in an unopened Amazon package in my basement, was written by Galam, who was the first to apply these renormalization methods to social issues and political science. His name was also well-known. He explained his findings to me and showed me a computer simulation of an election in which a minority's support must reach a threshold for its candidates to win.

Therefore, the same fallacy is propagated by political "scientists" in political discourse: you believe that since a candidate for an extreme right or left-wing party, for example, has the support of ten percent of the electorate, that party will win ten percent of the votes. No, these basic voters are "inflexible" and will only ever support their side. As non-Kosher persons may eat Kosher, certain flexible voters can also vote for that extreme group. These voters are the ones to look out for as they can increase the number of votes cast for the extreme party. Galam's models in political science created a wide range of surprising results, and his forecasts were far more accurate than the naïve consensus.

Chapter 3

How to Legally Own Another Person

A group of nomads known as the gyrovagues existed in the early years of the church when it was beginning to spread over Europe. They were roving monks who had no ties with any organization. Their kind of free-lance (and ambulatory) monasticism was viable because its members subsisted on beggarly work and the goodwill of townspeople who showed an interest in them. It is a poor kind of sustainability since it is difficult to call a community of celibate individuals sustainable because they cannot expand naturally and would need ongoing enrollment. However, its members were able to live because of assistance from the populace, who gave them food and makeshift housing.

They started going extinct sporadically around the fifth century and are now extinct. Gyrovagues were despised by the church and were outlawed by the councils of Chalcedon in the fifth century and Nicaea II about three hundred years later. Their biggest opponent in the West, Saint Benedict of Nursia, advocated a more institutionalized form of monasticism that ultimately won out thanks to his regulations that regulated the practice and included a hierarchy and strict abbot oversight. A monk's goods should be in the abbot's ownership, according to Rule 33 of Benedict's rules[i], which are organized like an instruction manual. Rule 70 prohibits furious monks from beating other monks.

What made them prohibited? Simply put, they were completely free. Not because of their resources, but rather because of their goals, they were financially comfortable and free. Ironically, they were able to get the equivalent of "f*** you money" by becoming beggars rather than by being members of the income-dependent class.

The last thing you would want if you were running an organized religion is complete independence. This chapter addresses the issue of workers, the nature of the company, and other institutions since total freedom is also very, very terrible for you if you have a business to manage.

In other words, every group wishes to deprive a certain proportion of the members of its membership of their freedom. How are these individuals owned by you? First, by training and psychological manipulation; second, by adjusting them to have some skin in the game, causing them to have something important to lose if they disobeyed authorities - something difficult to achieve with gyro-value beggars who flouted their hatred of worldly goods. Things are straightforward under mafia orders: created men (ordained men) may be wicked if the capo detects disloyalty, with a temporary stay in a car's trunk and an assurance that the boss would be present at their burial. Skin in the game takes on a subtler shape for those in different professions.

Ironically, even in ancient times when slavery was practiced, you could get along better with an employee than a slave.

Having a pilot

Let's imagine that you are the owner of a small airline. You consider the company to be a thing of the past because everything can be managed through a web of contractors. You are a very modern person who has attended numerous conferences and spoken to consultants. You're certain that doing so will be more effective.

Bob is a pilot with whom you have entered into a particular contract, in a well-defined, drawn-out legal agreement, for specific flights, commitments made far in advance, which includes a fine for non-performance. In case one of the pilots becomes ill, Bob provides a copilot and a backup. As part of an

Oktoberfest special, you will be running a scheduled flight to Munich tomorrow evening, and Bob is the hired pilot. The aircraft is packed with eager, low-cost passengers, some of whom started diets in preparation; they have been anticipating this enormous event of beer, pretzels, and sausage in laughter-filled hangars for a whole year.

At five o'clock in the afternoon, Bob calls to tell you that he and the copilot, well, they adore you. They won't fly the aircraft tomorrow, however, as you probably know. They received a proposal from a devoted Saudi Arabian Sheikh who wants to fly a special group of people to Las Vegas and requires Bob and his crew to manage the voyage. Bob's politeness, the fact that he had never touched alcohol in his life, his knowledge of fermented yogurt cocktails, and the Sheikh and his entourage's declaration that money was no object made them fall in love with Bob. The offer is so generous that it includes any fines associated with Bob breaking a competing contract.

You feel guilty. On these Oktoberfest flights, there are many attorneys, and even worse, there are many retired attorneys without hobbies who like suing as a means to pass the time, regardless of the result. Take into account the domino effect: if your plane doesn't take off, you won't have the means to bring the Munich-bound, beer-fattened passengers back, and you'll almost certainly miss many round trips. Rerouting travelers is expensive and uncertain.

After making a few calls, you discover that finding an academic economist with common sense and the capacity to comprehend what is happening is simpler than finding another pilot, which is an improbable occurrence. You own a lot of stock in a company that is now facing serious financial danger. You're certain that your business will fail.

You start to consider the possibility that such events would not be conceivable if Bob were your slave or another person who you owned. Slave? But hold on Employees that are in the business of being employees don't do what Bob just did! People who work for a livelihood as employees don't exhibit such opportunistic conduct. Contractors lack any real constraints and merely fear the law. However, staff needs to uphold their reputations. They may also be dismissed. People that like their jobs do so for a good reason. They like being paid!

People in employment tend to like the payroll's regularity and the special envelope that is sent to their desk on the final day of each month, without which they would behave like a newborn who hasn't had any breast milk. Then you see that you wouldn't be in this much difficulty if Bob had been an employee as opposed to that contractor arrangement that first looked to be cheaper.

But hiring personnel is costly... Even if you have nothing to do for them, you still have to pay them. You become less adaptable. They are far more expensive talent for talent. Paycheck lovers are sluggish, but they would never let you down in a crisis.

Employees are needed because they have a big stake in the outcome and are exposed to enough risk to serve as a deterrent and a punishment for irresponsible behavior like being late for work. Your purchase of reliability.

And many transactions are motivated by reliability. Because they want to make sure it is accessible in case they decide they wanted to use it on a whim, people of some means have country houses, which are inefficient compared to hotels or rentals. Never purchase when you can rent the three "Fs": what you Float, what you Fly, and what you...that something else," according to a saying. However, a lot of individuals also possess boats, airplanes, and other things.

A contractor might indeed have disadvantages, including potential financial penalties and reputational expenses. However, keep in mind that an employee will always be in greater danger. Furthermore, if someone is an employee, they will be risk-averse. They exhibit a certain level of domestication since they were formerly workers.
You are being provided with proof of submission by someone who has been employed for some time.

The routine of giving oneself independence for nine hours every day for years, arriving on time to an office, foregoing his schedule, and not beating anybody up are all indications of submission. You have a well-trained, obedient dog.
Employees are less risk-averse and worry more about being fired than contractors do about getting sued.

They will continue to be careful even after they stop being workers. The longer a person works for a firm, the more emotionally invested they get in it, and the more likely they are to leave on an "honorable departure."

The Company Person transitions from The Company Man

Therefore, if you reduce your tail risk, you also reduce your workers' tail risks. Or at least, they believe you to do that.

Firms now only remain in the top league by size (the so-called SP500) for 10 to fifteen years at most. Companies leave the SP500 via mergers or by cutting down on operations, both of which result in layoffs. However, the average length during the 20th century was more than 60 years. Large companies had a higher longevity rate; more individuals worked there throughout their lives. There formerly existed the concept of a corporate guy (restricting the gender here is appropriate as company men were almost all men).

The greatest definition of the corporate man, who predominated the 20th century, is someone whose identity is imbued with the imprint the corporation wishes to give him. He behaves appropriately, down to the language he employs, and the way he dresses. His social life is so intertwined with the business that quitting it would result in severe consequences, such as an exile from Athens under the Ostrakon. He goes out on Saturday evenings with other corporate guys and couples, telling jokes about the firm. In exchange, the company has an agreement to keep him on the books for as long as is practical, or until his required retirement, at which point he would go play golf with old coworkers while receiving a good pension. When big businesses were thought to live longer than nation-states and have extended lifespans, the system worked.

Our interpretation

A businessman is someone who has "skin in the game" and feels as if he stands to lose a lot if he doesn't act in a certain way.

If the businessman is, kind of, gone, the company's personality has taken his place as a result of both the gender's enlargement and the role's generalization. The reason is that the individual is no longer controlled by a business, but rather by something worse: the notion that he must be employable.

A company person is someone who has "skin in the game," or the mindset that they have a lot to lose if they lose their employment.

An employable person is ingrained in their field and is afraid of offending not just their company but also other possible employers.

By design, a worker is more valuable to the employer than the market when they work for the company than when they do so outside of it.

Perhaps by definition, an employable person is someone you won't discover in a history book since they are made to have no impact on how events turn out. They are not historically interesting by design.

The firm's theory of Coase

The real deal in terms of independent thought, rigor, creativity, and concepts that are relevant to and explain the reality around us is Ronald Coase, a great contemporary economist. Because of his strict writing style, he became famous for the Coase Theorem, a notion that he put out without using a single mathematical term but that is just as important as many things stated in mathematics.

In addition to his "theorem," Coase was the first to explain the purpose of companies. According to him, contracts might be too expensive to write since they include certain transaction costs. As a result, you incorporate your firm and recruit staff with clearly defined roles because you don't want to incur legal and organizational fees for every transaction. In a free market, pressures establish specialization and information flow through price points; yet, inside a corporation, these market forces are removed since they are more expensive to operate than they are beneficial. Thus, the company will have reached the ideal employee-to-contractor ratio, whereby having a certain number of employees, even if they are inherently inefficient, is preferable to having to invest a lot of resources in contract negotiations.

We can see that Coase halted just a few inches short of the idea of having skin in the game. He had no concept of risk, so he was unaware that an employee is a risk management tactic.

The risk management method used by Roman families, who typically had a slave serve as the household and estate's treasurer, would have been known to economists Coase and Shmoase if they had any interest in the ancient world. Why? Because you can punish a slave much more severely than a free person or a freedman, and you are not dependent on the legal system to do so. An unreliable or dishonest steward who diverts your estate's cash to Bithynia may bankrupt you. Having a slave do the steward role lowers your financial risk, but a slave has additional drawbacks.

Complexity

The contemporary world and complexity now enter the picture. Employees are more essential than ever for specialized activities in a world where items are being created by subcontractors with growing levels of expertise. This explains why, despite the appearance that things are running smoothly and efficiently in today's supposedly more efficient world of lower inventories and more subcontractors, mistakes are more expensive and delays are much longer than in the past. If you skip a step in a process, often the entire business shuts down. The whole chain may be stopped by a single delay.

Interesting Slave Ownership

Slave ownership by businesses has historically assumed quite odd shapes. The ideal slave overpays and is scared of falling out of favor. The ex-pat category was developed by multinational corporations as a kind of ambassador with a better level of life who would represent the company overseas and conduct its business abroad. With benefits and privileges like a country club membership, a driver, a nice company villa with a gardener, and a yearly trip back home with the family in first class, a bank in New York sends a married employee with his family to a foreign country, say a tropical country with cheap labor, and keeps him there for a few years, long enough for him to become addicted. In a system reminiscent of colonial times, he is paid far more than the "locals". He establishes friendships with other foreigners. He gradually wants to remain at the place for a longer period, but he is distant from the company's headquarters and has no other way of knowing his status inside the company except via signals. When it's time for a reorganization, he eventually pleads for a different place like a diplomat. Returning to the home office is giving up benefits, going back to the same basic wage, and being a complete slave. It also means going back to lower middle-class living in the suburbs of New York City, catching the commuter train or, heaven forbid, a bus, and eating sandwiches for lunch. When the huge boss ignores him, the individual feels afraid. Workplace politics will occupy 95% of the employee's thoughts, which is precisely what the firm wants. In the case of any intrigue, the big boss in the boardroom will have a backer.

Despite the price, all major firms had personnel with ex-pat status since it was a very successful tactic. Why? Because an employee's unit is more autonomous the further it is from headquarters, you want him to be a slave so he doesn't do anything odd on his own.

Non-Slave Workers

There is a group of workers that aren't slaves, but they make up a relatively tiny fraction of the workforce overall. They don't give a f*** about their reputation, at least not their business reputation, which makes them easy to spot.

After graduating from business school, I accidentally spent a year in a banking training program since the bank was unsure of my goals and experience and wanted me to work as an international banker. My most miserable experience in life occurred there when I was surrounded by very employable corporate personnel until I transferred to trading (with another business) and learned that some employees in a corporation weren't slaves.

One example is a salesman whose departure would result in a loss of revenue and, even worse, who, by taking some of the company's clients with him, would help a rival. Salespeople experienced tension with the company as a result of the company's attempts to depersonalize the relationship with the clients to separate the accounts from the salespeople, which was typically unsuccessful because people prefer to do business with other people and they stop doing so when a generic and polite person answers the phone in place of the warm and frequently exuberant salesperson-friend. The other trader was one for whom profits and losses, or P/L, were the only things that counted. Tradesmen and salesmen were rowdy; businesses had a love-hate relationship with them since they were only controllable when they were lucrative, in which case employers didn't want them.

I came to understand that successful trader may become so obnoxious that it was necessary to keep them away from the other workers. That is the cost of making people into profit centers by linking them to a certain P/L, which essentially made all other criteria irrelevant. I once threatened a trader who was verbally harassing the scared accountant in public, saying things like, "I am working hard to pay your wage" (suggesting that the firm's financial performance was not improved by the accounting). The people you meet while you're riding high are also the people you encounter when you're riding low, so it's not a big deal. I saw the man get some (more subtle) harassment from the same accountant before he was dismissed because he ultimately ran out of luck. You are free, but only to the extent of your most recent exchange. As I said previously, I changed companies to avoid the proto-company guy, and I was specifically informed that my job would end the moment I stopped meeting the P/L objective. Although I had no choice but to take the risk, because of the low level of knowledge among financial market participants at the time, I was obliged to participate in "arbitrage," low-risk transactions with little downside.

I remember being questioned about not wearing a tie, which was the equivalent of going barefoot down Fifth Avenue at the time. My go-to response was, "One part hubris, one part aesthetics, and one part convenience." If your business was successful, you could offer your managers everything you wanted since they wouldn't want to lose their positions.

Risk-takers may have erratic social behavior. Risk-taking is always linked to freedom, whether it originated from it or not. You take chances and sense historical significance. And those who take risks do so because they are by nature wild creatures.

Take note of the language component, which explains why merchants needed to be separated from the rest of the non-free, non-risk-taking population in addition to stylistic issues. In my day, only gang members and people who wanted to show that they were not slaves used profanity in public. However, traders used it like sailors, and I have continued to use it strategically in contexts other than my writing and family life. [4] People who use foul language on social media platforms (like Twitter) are, ironically, sending a costly message that they are independent and competent.

If you don't take risks to demonstrate your competence—and there aren't many such low-risk tactics—you don't indicate it. So, much as billionaires in Moscow wear blue jeans too big occasions to signify their power, swearing now is a status symbol. Even at banks, traders were shown to clients on company tours as if they were animals in a zoo, and it was commonplace to see a trader screaming at a broker while on the phone.

The "canaille" that etymologically links these individuals to dogs can thus be an indication of dog-like position and complete ignorance, but oddly, the greatest status, that of free man, is often shown by willingly adopting the mores of the lowest class[5]. Consider the fact that English "manners" do not apply to the nobility; rather, they are a middle-class phenomenon, and all of them are intended to domesticate people who need to be domesticated.

loss phobia

Let's start with the following:

What counts is what a person is terrified of losing, not what he or she has or doesn't have.

Therefore, individuals with more stakes are more vulnerable. Ironically, I've seen a lot of recipients of the so-called Nobel in Economics (the Riksbank Prize in Honor of Alfred Nobel) worry about losing a discussion while participating in them. Years ago, when I, a trader and an anonymous person, publicly referred to four of them as frauds, I saw that they were truly worried. Why were they concerned? Well, when you advance in that field, you get more uncomfortable because losing an argument with someone of lower status exposes you more than other people do.

Life advancement only works under certain circumstances. The director of the CIA is supposed to be the most powerful person in America, yet it turns out he is less powerful than a truck driver. Even having an adulterous romance was impossible for the man. You may endanger the lives of others while yet being a slave. The civil service is set up in this manner throughout.

Constantinople awaits

The autocrat offers the precise reverse of the public hotshot as a slave.

We are now seeing a developing conflict between several parties, including Vladimir Putin of Russia and the present "heads" of state members of the North Atlantic Treaty Organization (contemporary nations don't have heads, just individuals who speak a lot). Except for Putin, it is obvious that everyone else must carefully consider how every word may be misconstrued by the media. I have firsthand experience with this kind of insecurity. Putin, on the other hand, exudes a visible "I don't care," which in turn attracts more supporters from the electorate. He has the political equivalent of f***you money. In such a confrontation, Putin presents himself and behaves as a free person facing up against slaves who need committee approval, feel the need to conform their judgments to an instant rating, and more.

The effect of Putin's attitude on his supporters is mesmerizing, especially on the Orthodox Christians in Lebanon who lost the active protection of the Russian Czar in 1917 (against the Ottoman usurper of Constantinople) and now hope that Byzantium is returning about a century later, though the reincarnation is a little further north. It is far simpler to do business with the company's owner than with an employee who faces the prospect of losing his job the next year. Similarly, it is simpler to believe the word of an autocrat than that of a weak elected politician.

I learned that tamed (and sterilized) animals don't have a chance against a natural predator when seeing Putin compete against others. not one at all. The trigger, not the military might, is what matters.

The scenario did not much alter with the introduction of universal suffrage; up until recently, the electorate in so-called democracies consisted mostly of members of the upper class who gave little to no thought to the media. Ironically, however, more individuals might enter the pool of politicians with more social mobility, which could result in job loss. And over time, just like companies, you begin to assemble individuals who possess less bravery—individuals who are chosen for their lack of guts, much like in a typical organization.

Contrarily, the autocrat has greater freedom and, as in the unique instance of historic kings in tiny principalities, may have more stake in the improvement of the region than an elected politician whose primary duty is to demonstrate financial advantages. This is not the situation now when tyrants plunder the country and move riches to their Swiss bank accounts, as in the case of the Saudi Royal family, knowing that their time in power may be short.

Do not undermine bureaucracy.
More broadly:
You can't put your faith in people for important choices if their existence relies on qualitative "job appraisals" from someone in a higher position in the business.
Employees are trustworthy by nature, but they cannot be relied upon to make difficult choices or judgments that involve significant trade-offs. Additionally, according to firemen, they cannot handle situations until they work in the field. The employee's goal function is pretty straightforward, as we [saw/will see] with the payout function: do the duties that the employee's supervisor thinks are essential. The employee cannot stop and begins taking advantage of it if he is in the light fixture industry selling chandeliers and he learns the possibility of large prospects when he arrives at work in the morning, such as selling anti-diabetes goods to prediabetic Saudi Arabian tourists.

The employee is thus stranded should there be a change in the plan, even if they are here to avert an emergency. While the dispersion of tasks results in a significant dilution, which might produce this paralysis, there is another scale-related issue.

The impact of the Vietnam War was evident. Most people at the time (kind of) agreed that certain courses of action were stupid, but it was simpler to keep going than to turn back, especially because one can always come up with an argument for why doing so is preferable to stopping (the back fitting story of sour grapes now known as cognitive dissonance).

We are seeing the same issue with how the United States views Saudi Arabia. Since the World Trade Center assault on September 11, 2001, in which virtually all of the perpetrators were Saudi nationals, it has become obvious that someone in that non-partying country had some involvement in the incident. However, no bureaucrat made the best choice because of fear of oil interruptions; instead, the invasion of Iraq was approved because it seemed to be the easier option.

To put it mildly, since 2001, the strategy for combating Islamic terrorists has been entirely overlooking the disease—the proverbial "elephant in the room." Because it was not a route that was best for their job, even if it was ideal for the nation, policymakers and bureaucrats with sluggish minds foolishly allowed terrorism to flourish by ignoring the roots. We thus lost a generation because, while we were preoccupied with the use of sophisticated weapons and machinery, someone who attended grammar school in Saudi Arabia (our "ally") after September 11 is now an adult who has been brainwashed into believing and supporting Salafi violence, thus encouraged to finance it. Even worse, because of huge oil riches, the Wahabis have intensified the indoctrination of East and West Asians in their madrassas. It would have been simpler to concentrate on the Wahabi/Salafi teaching and the propagation of intolerance through which a Shiite, a Yazidi, or a Christian are deviant people rather than invading Iraq, bombing "Jihadi John" and other specific terrorists, and therefore multiplying these agents. But once again, it is not a choice that can be made by a group of bureaucrats following a set of predetermined duties.

Chapter 4

Life in the Simulation Machine

The nature of reality has been the subject of significant public inquiry and discussion. Elon Musk, the founder of Tesla and an active Twitter user, is one prominent intellectual who has expressed his opinion that it is statistically inevitable that our world will essentially consist of cascading green code. The probability that we are living in a simulation maybe 50-50, according to recent articles that have expanded on the initial concept to further narrow the statistical boundaries of the hypothesis.

Repetition of the assertions by notables such as Neil deGrasse Tyson, the director of the Hayden Planetarium and America's favorite scientific popularizer, has given them some credibility. But there have also been doubters. According to physicist Frank Wilczek, our cosmos contains too much-wasted complexity for it to be accurately replicated. Complexity needs effort and time to build. Why would a conscious, wise reality-maker spend so much energy on making our world more complicated than it has to be? Despite being speculative, the query could still be necessary.

Sabine Hossenfelder, a physicist and science communicator, is one person who has claimed that the issue is not scientific in the first place. We can't verify or refute the simulation hypothesis since it doesn't lead to a falsifiable prediction, hence it isn't worth studying.

However, I think that all of these analyses and debates on the simulation hypothesis have overlooked a crucial aspect of scientific investigation: straightforward empirical evaluation and data gathering. We need to look at the fact that we already have computers running a variety of simulations for lower-level "intelligence" or algorithms to comprehend whether we are living in a simulation. For simplicity, let's think of this intelligence as any nonhuman character in any video game we like playing, but in reality, our thought experiment would apply to any algorithm running on any computer device. Because the proof we're seeking is "experienced" by all computer programs, basic or complicated, operating on all computers, slow or fast, we don't even need the intelligence to be aware or particularly complex.

Every piece of computer gear leaves a trace of its presence in the simulated environment in which it is used. The speed of the processor is this artifact. The only and unavoidable artifact of the hardware supporting us in our world, if we were to imagine for a moment that we were a software program running on a computer, would be the processor speed. The only other rules we would encounter are those of the simulation or piece of software we are using. These would be the rules of the game if we were a Sim or Grand Theft Auto character. But regardless of the game's rules, everything we do would likewise be limited by the processor speed. The processor speed would affect the simulation's activities regardless of how thorough the simulation is.

Naturally, this interference of processing speed into the reality of the algorithm being performed occurs even at the most basic level in computer systems. The processing speed imposes a physical reality on the operation that is separate from the simulated reality of the operation itself, even at the most basic level of simple operations like addition or subtraction.

Here is an easy illustration. It would take a 64-bit processor the same amount of time to subtract, for example, 7,862,345 from 6,347,111 as it would subtract two from one (granted all numbers are defined as the same variable type). Seven million is a very huge number in the simulated world, whereas one is a comparably extremely tiny amount. The fact that these two integers are scaled differently does not affect the processor's actual operation. In our case, both subtractions are one operation and would finish at the same time. The distinction between a "simulated" or abstract world of programmed mathematics and a "real" or physical world of microprocessor operations is now quite evident.

The processing speed of operations per second will be seen, felt, experienced, and documented as a byproduct of the underlying physical computing equipment in the abstract realm of programmed mathematics. Any operation that is unaffected by the operation in the simulated world will have this artifact as an extra component. The time it takes to execute one operation on a variable up to a maximum that is equal to the variable's memory container size would be the value of this extra component of the operation. In an eight-bit computer, for example, this would be 256, to simplify. All numbers up to the upper limit will have the same value for this extra component. Therefore, other than if it turns out to be the maximum container size, the extra hardware component will be unimportant for all activities inside the simulated world. The only time the processor speed can be measured by the observer within the simulation is when it acts as an upper bound.

If our reality is a simulation, then our universe ought to include such a thing. Now that we have some of this artifact's characteristics defined, we can start looking for more of them throughout the universe.

Every operation includes the artifact as an extra component. It is unaffected by the size of the variables being operated on and has no impact on the simulated reality until a maximum variable size is seen.

The artifact appears as a cap in the virtual environment.

The underlying mechanistic principles of the simulated world cannot account for the artifact. Within the rules of the simulated world, it must be taken as a given or assumed.

The anomaly's or artifact's effects are irreversible. Without exceptions

It is obvious what the artifact presents in our reality now that we are familiar with some of its distinguishing characteristics. The speed of light seems to be the artifact.

Space is to our universe what numbers are to any computer-generated simulation of reality. Simply put, operations on the variable space are what are occurring while matter moves across space. If the matter is traveling, say, at the speed of one thousand miles per second, then one thousand miles of space are being altered, or acted upon, each second. A maximum limit on the container size for space on which one operation can be performed would be a telltale sign of the hardware artifact within the simulated reality "space" if there were any hardware powering the simulation known as "space," of which matter, energy, you, me, and everything is a part. Such a restriction would show up as a maximum speed in our universe.

The speed of light is the highest. We don't know what hardware is operating the simulation of our world or what characteristics it has, but we do know that if the CPU ran one operation per second, the memory container size for the variable space would be around 300,000 kilometers.

This leads us to a fascinating conclusion regarding the character of space in our universe. If we are, as it seems, in a simulation, then space is an intangible characteristic that has been programmed. It's not true. Similar to the seven million and one in our example, it is only a new abstract representation on a memory block of the same size. These are just symbols for up, down, forward, backward, 10 miles, and millions of kilometers. The amount of the causal effect of any action on the variable "space" is represented by the speed at which anything is traveling through space (and, therefore, altering space or conducting an operation on space). Given that the universe computer does one operation each second, this causal influence cannot go beyond around 300,000 kilometers.

We can now see that the speed of light satisfies every requirement for a hardware artifact that we have seen in our computer designs. It is viewed as a maximum limit, it is constant regardless of observer (simulated) speed, it is not explicable by universe physics, and it is unalterable. We exist in a virtual world, as shown by the speed of light.

However, this is hardly the only sign that our world is a simulation. The most important clue may have been hidden right before our eyes. Alternatively, behind them. We must return to our empirical analysis of the simulations we are aware of to comprehend what this crucial hint is. Consider a role-playing game (RPG) character, such as a Sim or the protagonist of Grand Theft Auto. At many different levels, the algorithms that depict the character and the gaming world in which the character plays are interwoven. The character may interact with the environment without a visual projection of its point of view, even if we believe that the character and the environment are distinct.

The algorithms project and predict the behavior of both the environment and the character by taking into consideration several environmental factors as well as several character state variables. What we see on the screen or the visual projection, is for our benefit. For us to feel as if we are playing the game, certain program variables are projected subjectively. The audiovisual simulation of the game functions as a built-in subjective interface for our benefit, effectively acting as a simulation controller. The only purpose of the integrated subjective interface is to benefit us. Movies may be used as a thinking experiment in a similar way. Movies often adopt the viewpoint of characters and attempt to depict events from their point of view. Whether a specific movie scene does that or not, the entire experience of the film—what is displayed on the screen and heard via the speakers—serves no function for the characters in the movie. It is only for our advantage.

We have been pondering the topic of why we need awareness pretty much from the beginning of philosophy. What function does it fulfill? Well, once we accept the simulation concept, the aim is simple to extrapolate. An integrated, subjective interface between the self and the rest of the cosmos is consciousness, which combines the five senses. Its purpose as an "experience" is the only logical explanation for its existence. That is its main purpose in existence. It may or may not include components that provide any kind of evolutionary benefit or another benefit. The fact that it is all combined as an experience means that its main purpose must be to serve as an experience. A single experience is a resource- and information-demanding to have emerged as a competitive advantage. An experience or qualia may be best understood as existing for the sole purpose of existing as an experience.

Nothing in philosophy or science—no postulates, hypotheses, or laws—would foretell the advent of this phenomenon that we refer to as awareness. Its presence is not mandated by natural principles, and it doesn't seem to provide humans with any evolutionary benefits either. There are just two possibilities for how it may exist. The first is that the development of the experience known as consciousness is selected for by evolutionary mechanisms that we are unaware of or have not yet postulated. The second is that the experience is a purpose we fulfill, a thing we make, and something we do as people. Who are we designing this for? How do they get the results of our qualia-generating algorithms? We are unsure. But we do make it, that much is certain. Its existence is known. We have no other certainty but that. And that no widely accepted explanation explains why we need it.

Thus, we are producing awareness, a good that we seem to have no purpose for but which is an experience and must therefore function as an experience. The only reasonable conclusion is that this commodity has another purpose.

One argument against this school of thought is that, unlike the RPG characters in, for example, Grand Theft Auto, we have direct experience with the qualia. Why are we experiencing it if it's a product meant for someone else? The protagonists in Grand Theft Auto do, in reality, feel some of their existence's qualia. However, there is a gray region between the player and the empty character where elements of both the player and the character merge to form some kind of awareness. The experiences of the characters and the player of the game are significantly different.

Players experience some of the pleasures and disappointments that the character is supposed to feel. The effects of the player's actions are felt by the character. Although there is just a very basic link between the player and the avatar, the lines between them are already blurred thanks to virtual reality technology. We experience gravity while riding a roller coaster as a character, for example, with an Oculus VR headset.

What is the source of gravity? It is there somewhere between the character riding the roller coaster and our brains, which are taking up residence in the character's "mind." It is conceivable that this transitional area might expand in the future. A more information-rich version of the qualia may be projected to another mind for whose benefit the experience of consciousness initially came into being, while we are undoubtedly experiencing some very little portion of the qualia as we experience the environment and produce them.

There you have it, then. Consciousness may be explained most simply as an experience that is being formed by our body, but not for us. We are machines that produce qualia. We are here to provide integrated audiovisual products, much like the protagonists in Grand Theft Auto. Additionally, much like the protagonists in Grand Theft Auto, our product is probably intended for someone who is living her life through us.

What are the ramifications of this significant discovery? We can't ask Elon Musk any more questions, to start with. Ever. Second, we should not lose sight of the true nature of the simulation theory. The most elaborate conspiracy theory exists. The conspiracy theory that claims that everything is phony and a plot to deceive us, except for nothing, is the mother of all conspiracies. Our darkest nightmares about strong powers influencing our lives in secret have finally materialized. Yet in its revelation, this complete helplessness and consummate duplicity leave us with no escape. All we can do is accept the simulation's actuality and make the most use of it.

Chapter 5

Inequality and Skin in the Game

Both inequality and inequality exist.

The first is the inequality that individuals allow, such as when one compares their comprehension to that of heroes like Einstein, Michelangelo, or the reclusive scientist Grisha Perelman, to whom one has no trouble admitting a significant excess. This holds for businesspeople, artists, warriors, heroes, Bob Dylan, Socrates, the current neighborhood star chef, and any reputable Roman Emperor, like Marcus Aurelius; in other words, anyone for whom one may naturally be a "fan." You may admire them and want to be like them, but you don't dislike them. The second is the inequality that people find intolerable because the subject seems to be just like you, except that he has been taking advantage of the system by engaging in rent-seeking and obtaining unjustified privileges. Although he may have a Russian girlfriend, for example, he is exactly the kind of person you cannot possibly like. The other group includes bankers, wealthy government officials, ex-senators who promote the terrible corporation Monsanto, clean-shaven CEOs who wear ties and talking heads on television who get generous bonuses. Not only are you envious of them, but you are also offended by their celebrity and feel resentment when you see their luxury or even moderately costly automobile. They reduce your size.

The sight of a wealthy slave may have something off-putting about it. In this interesting piece, author Joan Williams demonstrates that the working class looks up to the wealthy as role models. She quotes Michèle Lamont, author of The Dignity of Working Men, who conducted a thorough interview with blue-collar Americans and discovered that there was animosity among professionals but, surprisingly, not among the wealthy.

It is reasonable to assume that the American public, in fact, the whole public, despises those who get a high income or, more specifically, salarymen who earn a high salary. This is seen in other nations as well: a few years ago, a third of Swiss voters—of all people—voted in support of legislation restricting management wages. However, the same Swiss have a certain amount of respect for wealthy businesspeople and others who became famous in different ways.

Furthermore, money is seen as zero-sum in nations where it derives from rent-seeking, political patronage, or what is known as regulatory capture (in which the powerful utilize regulations to defraud the public or red tape to stifle competition). What Paul gives to Peter is taken from him. Someone is gaining wealth at the cost of other people. People can readily understand that someone becoming wealthy is not taking money out of their pocket; in fact, they may even be putting some in it, especially in nations like the U.S. where riches may be created via devastation. On the other hand, inequality is a zero-sum game by definition.

Both static and dynamic elements

One of the problems with economists (especially those who have never worked in the real world) is that they struggle mentally with moving objects and are unable to understand that moving objects have different characteristics from still objects. This may seem trivial, but if you are still not convinced, reread Chapter [3] on IYIs. Because of this, most of them are unfamiliar with complexity theory and fat tails; they also struggle (severely) with the conceptual and mathematical intuitions necessary for more in-depth probability theory. Blindness to ergodicity, which we shall describe later, is, in my view, the greatest indicator of a true scholar who knows the world from an academic hack who engages in ritualistic paper writing.

Let's define a few terms:

Static inequality is just a moment in time and does not represent what will happen to you throughout your life.

Consider that more than half of all Americans will spend a year in the top ten percent and that 10% of Americans will spend at least one year in the top 1%[1]. For Europe, which is more stagnant but ostensibly more equal, this is not the same. A third of the richest Europeans were the richest centuries ago, whereas just 10% of the richest 500 Americans or families were so thirty years ago; more than 60% of those on the French list were heirs. It was recently discovered that the situation in Florence is far worse than previously thought: the same few families have maintained their fortune for five centuries.

Dynamic (ergodic) inequality considers one's complete past and future lives.

Raising the status of those at the bottom alone won't produce dynamic equality; you also need to force

the wealthy to rotate or expose themselves to the prospect of generating an opportunity.
By putting the wealthy in danger of leaving the one percent (via "skin in the game"), society may become more egalitarian.
or, in a more mathematical way
Dynamic equality presupposes an unabsorbable Markov chain.
Our situation is more serious than just economic mobility. Mobility entails the potential for financial success. Being wealthy does not guarantee continued wealth due to the no-absorbing barrier situation.

More mathematically speaking now
Ergodicity is restored through dynamic equality, which makes temporal and ensemble probability interchangeable.
As we shall show, ergodicity cancels the majority of the most important psychological tests relating to probability and reason, which is what we mentioned is alien to the intelligentsia. Obtain a cross-section of the American population. Consider the minority of millionaires in the one percent; some are obese, some are tall, and others are funny. A significant portion of the population also belongs to the lower

middle class, and there are many school-based yoga teachers, bakers, gardeners, spreadsheet theorists, dance instructors, and piano tuners. Count the proportions in each income or wealth category (note that income inequality is flatter than that of wealth). Perfect ergodicity states that each of us, if we lived forever, would spend the proportion of our time in the economic conditions of different groups within that entire cross-section: on average, for, say, a century, we would spend sixty years in the lower middle class, ten years in the upper middle class, twenty years in the blue-collar class, and perhaps one year in the one percent. (Technical comment: What we can refer to as imperfect ergodicity here means that each of us has long-term, ergodic probabilities that vary slightly between individuals: your probability of ending in the one percent range may be higher than mine, but no state will have a probability of zero for me and no state will have a transition probability of one for you.)

An absorbing condition is the precise opposite of complete ergodicity. The word "absorption" refers to particles that, upon contact with an obstruction, either absorb or adhere to it. Once within an absorbing barrier, it's impossible to escape, whether it's for good or harm. A person becomes wealthy by some procedure, and once there, as they say, he remains wealthy. And if someone falls into the lower middle class (from above), he or she will never have the opportunity to rise to the upper class and become affluent, should they want to do so. As a result, they will have good reason to dislike the wealthy. In countries like France, where the state is friendly with big firms and prevents its executives and stockholders from suffering such a drop, it even supports their rise, you'll observe that those at the top tend to experience minimal downward mobility there.

Additionally, if there is no downside for some, there is also no upside for others.

Consider for the time being that route dependency, the subject of Part X, is caused by an absorbing state—staying affluent.

Pikketism and the Mandarin Class Uprising

There is a class that is sometimes referred to as the Mandarins, after the fictitious memoirs of French novelist Simone de Beauvoir, and named after the Ming dynasty intellectuals who gave the high Chinese language its name. I had known about it my whole life, but I just recently realized how prominent and harmful it is after seeing how people responded to the writings of French economist Thomas Piketty.

Piketty wrote an ambitious book on Capital as Karl Marx's successor. I was given the book while it was still in French and had no audience outside of France because I thought it was admirable when individuals published their original, non-mathematical social science work in book form. The book Capital in the 21st Century asserted vehemently that inequality was alarmingly rising, added to a theory explaining why capital tended to command an excessive rate of return relative to labor and explained how the absence of redistribution and dispossession would bring about the end of the world. Anyone who has seen the emergence of what is referred to as the "knowledge economy" (or anyone who has made investments in general) understands that the hypothesis about the increase in the return of capital in proportion to labor was demonstrably incorrect. However, there was something much, much worse than a scholar being in error.

I soon learned that the techniques he used were flawed: Picketty's instruments did not support the claims he made on the growth in inequality. I quickly produced two pieces, one of which I co-authored with Raphael Douady and which we published in Physica A: Statistical Mechanics and Applications, on the way to quantify inequality, which is to take ownership of, say, the top 1% and track changes in it. The problem is that, when assessed as a whole, Europe's inequality is greater than its component nations' average inequality, and the distortion becomes worse with more severe processes. The Gini coefficient, a tool used by academics to gauge inequality, has the same flaw, and I produced another study on it. I insisted on presenting the results in theorem form because one cannot contest a formally proved theorem without calling into question his understanding of mathematics. Overall, the papers contained enough theorems and proofs to make them about as infallible a piece of work as one can have in science.

Because economists who dealt with inequality were unfamiliar with it, these mistakes went unnoticed. Rich individuals were in the tails of the distribution, which is how inequality is defined as the disproportion of the tail's role. [2] The winner-take-all effect and the degree of systemic inequality increase as we get farther away from the tin-tailed Mediocristan approaches economists were taught. Remember that winner-take-all effects, the kind outlined in The Black Swan, dominate the wealth process. People who have privileges tend to be locked in their condition of entitlement as a result of any kind of wealth process control, which is often launched by bureaucrats. Therefore, the ideal option in the United States was to let the system decimate the powerful.

It's how people respond to an issue, not the problem itself. Even worse than the Piketty errors was learning how that Mandarin class works. Their activities resembled false news because they were so enthused by the growth in inequality. When Piketty discussed Balzac and Jane Austen, economists were so enthused that they commended him for his "erudition," which is the equivalent of praising a briefcase-carrying person as a weightlifter. And when they did acknowledge my findings, it was to label me "arrogant" (keep in mind that the tactic of using theorems is that they can't say I was incorrect; so, they resorted to using the word "arrogant," which is a type of scientific flattery). Even Paul Krugman said that "you're very likely mistaken" if you believe you have identified an evident empirical or logical flaw in Piketty. He completed his assignment! When I saw [iv] in person, he skirted the fault when I pointed it out to him; this wasn't necessarily out of malice, but most likely because, as he admitted, probability and combinatorics escaped him.

Now suppose that people like Krugman and Piketty have no drawbacks to their existence since reducing inequality advances them in society. They will keep being paid as long as the French state or the academic system doesn't collapse. Not them, but Donald Trump is in danger of eventually eating in a soup kitchen.

Builder Envies Cobbler Envy does not span so many social levels or great distances. As we observed in the writings of Williams and Lamont, the envy-driven sentiments that are often not from the lower classes, concerned with improving their status, but rather with those of the clerical class. Simply put, it seems that the case was overwhelmingly backed by tenured academics and government employees, as well as university instructors (who have already arrived). I was persuaded by the dialogues that these counterfactual upwards (i.e., compare themselves to others who are wealthier) individuals want to displace the wealthy. Like many communist movements, the bourgeois or clerical classes often adopt the viewpoint first.

In his Rhetoric, Aristotle claimed that jealousy is something you are more likely to experience in your own family. Lower classes are more likely to feel envy for their relatives or the middle class than for the wealthy, according to Aristotle. This line in the Rhetoric is where the idiom Nobody is a prophet in his place making envy a geographical matter, which is wrongly attributed to Jesus, first appears in Luke and is repeated in Mark. Building on Hesiod, Aristotle said that "cobblers envy cobblers" and "carpenters envy carpenters." Later, La Bruyere noted that the same skill, art, and condition might all include envy.

Therefore, unlike Lamont, I doubt Piketty bothered to ask French blue-collar workers what they want. I'm sure they wouldn't want to bring down a wealthy, unknowable billionaire; instead, they could ask for a new dishwasher or a speedier train for their commute. However, as was the case before the French Revolution, individuals might pose concerns and characterize enrichment as theft, in which case the blue-collar class would once again demand that heads be rolled.

[1] " .," Rhetoric 1388a, citing Aeschylus, frag. 304 as the primary source.

[2] La Bruyere: People who share the same skill, art, and circumstance are the only ones who experience jealousy and emulation.

Shamata, Data

Another takeaway from Piketty's ambitious book is that it had a ton of graphs and tables. But we see from experts in the real world that data is not always rigorous. As a probability expert, I intentionally omitted statistics from The Black Swan (other than for illustrative reasons) because I believe that people tend to overstuff stories with facts in the absence of a compelling argument. Furthermore, empiricism is often confused with data overload. When one is correct, just a little amount of important evidence is required, especially when it comes to disconfirmation empiricism or counterexamples to rules: only one point is enough to demonstrate the existence of black swans.

Statistics, probability, and data science are primarily forms of reasoning that are fueled by observations and the lack of observations. The key data points for many ecosystems are those at the extremes; they are by definition few, and it is sufficient to concentrate on those few but significant data points to obtain a sense of the narrative. If you want to prove that someone is wealthier than, say, $10 million, all you have to do is demonstrate the $50 million in his brokerage account; you don't even need to detail every piece of furniture in his home or do a count of the silver spoons in his cupboard. So I've learned from experience that something is very suspect when you purchase a big book with a ton of graphs and tables used to establish a point. It indicates that something went wrong with the distillation! Such tables are another attempt to replace the real with the complex, but to the general public and those without a background in statistics, they seem convincing. For instance, scientific writer Steven Pinker accomplished this with his book The Better Angels of Our Nature, which examines the reduction of violence across contemporary human history. When my colleague Pasquale Cirillo and I examined his "data," we discovered that either he didn't understand his numbers (which he didn't), or he had a narrative in mind and kept adding charts without realizing that statistics isn't about data but distillation, rigor, and avoid being fooled by randomness - but regardless, the general public of IYI colleagues initially found it impressive.

Civil service ethics

People who like bureaucracy and the state sometimes struggle to see the distinction between having wealthy individuals hold public office and those same individuals becoming wealthy; once again, it is the dynamics and order that count. Rich individuals who hold public office have shown some signs that they are not completely incompetent. Success may, of course, be attributed to chance, but there is at least some indication that they have some real-world experience. This is contingent on the individual having some stake in the outcome, and it is preferable if they suffered a blowout and had at least once faced the pain of losing a portion of their riches.

A decent guideline for society is to require persons who enter public service to promise never to earn more from the private sector than a certain amount in the future; the remaining amount should be paid for by the taxpayer. This would guarantee honesty in "service," when workers are allegedly underpaid due to their psychological benefits from helping society. You don't become a Jesuit priest so that Goldman Sachs will hire you later, after your eventual defrocking, given the erudition and the masterful control of casuistry typically associated with the

Society of Jesus. This would demonstrate that they are not in the public sector as an investment strategy.

Currently, the majority of public officials prefer to remain in their positions, except for those who work in sensitive sectors that are under the authority of industry, such as the agro-alimentary sector, banking, aerospace, and anything involving Saudi Arabia.

Currently, a public servant may create regulations that benefit industry, like banking, and then go to work for J.P. Morgan where they can earn back multiples of the difference between their present pay and the going rate. (Recall that regulators are motivated to create regulations as complicated as possible so that their knowledge may eventually be recruited at a higher rate.)

Therefore, there is an inherent inducement in the public service: you serve a business, like Monsanto, and they look after you afterward. They merely do it because it is essential to maintain such a system and urge the next man to follow the rules, not because of any feeling of honor. Tim Geithner, an IYI cum scoundrel with whom I share a Calabrese barber,